DUE SOUTH

An Antarctic Journal

John Kelly

First published in 2004 by
Signal Books Limited
36 Minster Road
Oxford
OX4 1LY
www.signalbooks.co.uk

A catalogue record for this book is available from the British Library

ISBN 1-902669-90-8 Paper

All photographs and drawings by John Kelly, except p.59 and p.61, by William
Jameson from *The Wandering Albatross* (Rupert Hart-Davis, 1958)
Cover Design: Devdan Sen
Typesetting: Devdan Sen
Cover Images: John Kelly

Printed by the Alden Press, Oxford

PREFACE

This book is the result of a journal kept while in Maritime Antarctica during the southern summer of 2003. For much of this time I was based at Signy, a small island within the South Orkneys, in Maritime Antarctica to the north of the Weddell Sea. This island serves as one of the remote scientific research stations of the British Antarctic Survey, which forms the main British presence in the South Polar Region, covering a wide-ranging area of scientific enquiry. This includes meteorology, global warming issues, geology and glacial activity, botany and biology.

As selected artist, I was to produce a visual diary and conduct studies of the landscape and wildlife. It was from this work that I wanted to create an impression of what being in the Antarctic was actually like.

For most of us, mention of Antarctica evokes scenes of great white expanses and spell-binding beauty within a landscape of glaciers and ice sheets.

Some years ago I visited the Maritime Museum at Greenwich to see the exhibition 'South', based on the early exploration of the Southern Polar area. Behind the black and white photographs of the great ice sheets, with the stark outlines of equipment and vessels, I came upon the small cases of belongings and letters that had been saved from these expeditions. These objects told a story that seemed detached from the harsh scenes of the photographs; they came from a sanctum that these men had created when confronted with the extreme conditions against which they had fought. There seemed to be two contrasting impressions of Antarctica: a visual and cruel outer landscape and an inner silent area of the mind.

My own experience of Antarctica involved a number of confrontations, including not only traversing the ice cap but also the sea journey itself. Antarctica's isolation and the dangers of the Southern Ocean go hand in hand; these turbulent waters give a fitting preparation for the White Continent that lies beyond. Confronting a storm within these high latitudes, like the confrontation with the ice sheet itself, signals that time of inner consolidation when we find solace within that 'silent sea'. There is something within the human spirit that creates this haven when we are faced with such scenes of the sublime—the source of an inner strength.

Much of the contents of this journal comes from that 'silent sea'. On many occasions during my time in the south I found that the reality of Antarctica was too great and led to a sort of sensory over-exposure. Witnessing the sublime on such a scale necessitated an avenue of escape, and so it was that I turned to the sketch book and journal.

This book and the exhibitions to follow would not have been possible without the support and encouragement of a number of people. My thanks go to Professor David Walton of the British Antarctic Survey (BAS) for guiding me in the early stages of my application to go to the south and particularly for his wisdom in suggesting the Signy base as the most appropriate for my work. I would also like to thank Gordon Rankmore of the Natural History Museum (NHM) for seeing the potential of my application at such an early stage and for offering support to my application to travel with BAS.

I would also like to thank Paul McKee of the Cheltenham Museum and Kate White of the Pitt-Rivers Museum in Oxford for their support, and Bob Headland of the Scott Polar Institute in Cambridge for his help and advice concerning the use of the archives.

There are many individuals who have helped in this project from both the BAS and NHM, and without their assistance the whole experience would not have been so enjoyable or fulfilling. Fond memories go to my colleagues on Signy Island with whom I shared the glorious isolation, namely Rod Strachan, Richard Borthwick, Karen De Boer, Peter Boelen, Mike Dunn and Aki Takahashi. Thanks go to Mike and Aki for allowing me to share those delightful days among the penguin colonies and to Rod for enabling me to see the entire island in one day.

Finally, I would like to express my gratitude to Southern and South East Arts for funding the Antarctica Project.

John Kelly
Brighton, 2004

To Dinah, Liberty and Asa

'Beyond this flood
a frozen continent lies
dark and wilde,
beat with perpetual storms
of whirlwind and dire hail,
which on firm land
thaws not, but gathers heap,
and ruin seems of ancient pile;
all else deep snow and ice.'

John Milton, 1608-1672.

Deep Field

In 1996 the Hubble Space Telescope concentrated its eye upon a single dot in space to introduce a further forty billion galaxies to our small planet, within an area that became known as Hubble 'deepfield'.

In Antarctica they also talk of deepfield. Within the cold wastes, deepfield lies remote. These are the areas where the trail of men fleetingly disturbs the purity of surface and time is broken underfoot.

13 December 2002

Thoughts of the Southern Ocean

Sending out ropes
upon the great white whale.

28 December 2002

The Journey

Brize Norton. Flight to the Falkland Islands.

Port Stanley. Voyage south on the RRS *Ernest Shackleton.*

16 January 2003

Sketch the first

In the carcass of an old
land,
limestone grey and midsummer
yellow cut lizard backs
across the faded skin
of the earth.

Here, battle was fought
within
some ancient field,
whilst all is now still
save
the distant wave.

Falkland Islands. 21 January 2003

Days at Sea (I)

As I watch the ship being prepared for departure from Port Stanley, engines are started, emitting large plumes of black smoke into the clear air of the bay. The hoisting crane is lowered to its resting place upon the deck and the closed doors of the hold. Dolphins play near to the ship as we move out towards the 'narrows' beyond the calm waters and finally to the open sea. I make my way to the bridge and among the array of equipment and computer screens I notice an image appearing from the orbiting satellite as it tracks south over Argentina and Chile. Weather and sea ice conditions display a clear picture of our journey to the Weddell Sea. The sea ice is thick within the polar ocean, but here is a clear cut that will take us safely south. Had this level of information been at hand, Shackleton would not have made the decision to sail due south, but would have gone east to the safety of a land journey.

The Falklands archipelago consists of numerous flat, low-lying islands that barely rise above one hundred feet. It is a monotonous landscape which, like all flat lands, draws the eye to full skies and an immense volume that forms the air of the south. From the boat I can see beyond the islands to the distant ocean as it disturbs the smoothness of the horizon. Sea swell and individual waves begin to fill the view before us with the white flecks of breakers. Binoculars only emphasise the line of activity: a deep blue shimmering strip of ocean energy. To the south and east the grey density of the mountains rises above the sparseness of the grasslands. A spine of rock defies the relentless winds, the dominant forces of these desolate lands.

In the late afternoon the islands appear to be upon a cushion of light and lie suspended above the cool of the ocean surface as we move out from their shelter into the open sea. By evening we are within the spell of the Southern Ocean with the arrival of the first albatross.

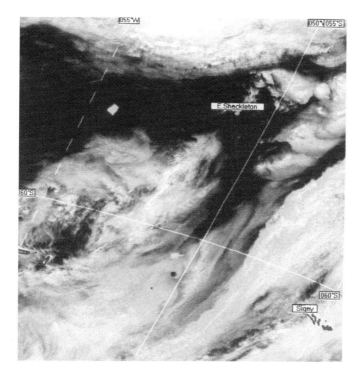

Sketch the second

Almost by chance,
a glance to port
and there
the effortless glide
on wings too slender.

And later that day,

in low flight,
the occasional motion of wings.
Close to the ocean skin
the great bird passes
over the slate grey water.

Southern Ocean. 22 January 2003

Days at Sea (II)

I stand on the uppermost deck facing due south beneath a blue sky. Ahead, a low bank of cloud skirts the horizon. Tantalisingly, Antarctica lies below that line of convecting air. Fragmenting cumuli pass to the west. A glimpse at the weather chart tells us that the main cyclonic system is deepening to the east. These passing clouds are being drawn into that bigger system. The ocean surface is now deep blue and a lifting breeze disturbs and picks up small breakers, interrupting the great gestation of the southern swell. Like the small scurrying clouds, these flecks of white water are but small players in the immense circulations that constantly pulsate within and above the Southern Ocean.

22.00 hrs. Early evening and the temperature is now dropping as we close on the zone of convergence. Cold waters of the Antarctic are flowing to meet the warmer northern currents. Albatrosses skim the steel grey waters, occasionally rising to observe us before veering out to sea to drop within the ocean swell. A pack of orca patrols to the west.

24 January 2003.I awake to a grey overcast day with variable wind and a slight swell. In the haze of early morning the silver grey outline of the first iceberg appears in the cold light of mid distance. This spectre, so full of weighty omen, causes unfamiliar thoughts to pass through my mind. During the morning the sea's aspect changes, its grey surface becoming busy with the arrival of 'growlers' and broken bergs so that my body temperature drains away before these frosty wrecks. White veiled, they pass like a procession of sheeted furniture. A sense of dislocation sets in throughout the day, and with evening the moon and planets seem out of their customary alignment.

This is a strange place.

19.30 hrs. Unerringly calm and waveless, with only the sound of the ship's engines carrying over the waters. Still the silent procession of icebergs drifting slowly to the north. Occasionally a disturbance of the water surface by seal or penguin, below an empty sky. Ahead, within the shadow of cloud, lie the dark outlines of the large ice shelves between us and the Weddell Sea.

In the failing light of day the exhalation of whale spout in the mid distance, like the release of steam from the cold waters. The crazed spirit belching from some sunken vent; a sea fumarole heralding the spirits of the south. A Scylla and Charybdis of the South Atlantic.

Southern Ocean. 23 January 2003

Arrival at Signy

Signy, lying to the south of Coronation Island, forms part of the Orkneys. A remote and windswept archipelago gripped for eight long winter months in the frozen hold of the Antarctic and released for the remainder of the year to form a home for the wildlife populations of seals, penguins and numerous seabirds.

Base at Signy Island consists of a collection of small buildings that skirt the eastern shoreline of Factory Cove.

10.30 hrs. We arrive in Borge Bay amid extensive sea ice. Brilliant light emanates from the ice and snow surfaces as we drift slowly towards Signy. Unable to penetrate the ice to base, we board a small craft and are dropped near to the beacon on Bernstein Rocks.

Hours later, I return to these rocks to watch the departure of the *Ernest Shackleton*. Dwarfed by the icebergs now entering the bay, the ship gradually makes its way to the open waters of the Southern Ocean.

Orcadian Days

The Signy Island Journals
25 January to 8 March 2003

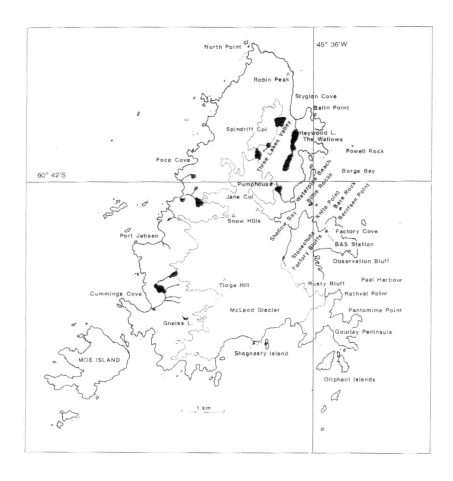

Map of Signy Island 60° 42'S 45° 36'W. giving the place names used
in the text

Sketch the third

> High
> upon the ice cap,
> away from the sounds
> of sea
> and headland of rock,
> this seems a silent place.

27 January 2003

Signy Island Journal (I)

28 January 2003. Sombre Lake and the Ice Cap.

8.30 hrs. We depart from base to catch the low tide across the 'shallows' of scattered rock that has been washed down from the Orwell Glacier and the adjacent Limestone Valley. Numerous fur seals and a group of elephant seals lie over the nearby areas of ancient riverbank like beaten rugs. Entering Three Lakes Valley beneath low cloud we are followed closely by the swooping and diving of terns and skuas as we pass the nesting areas.

Approaching the beach at Stygian Cove we disturb the slumbering fur seals. It is a beach of broken moraine littered with whalebone that has been discoloured by time to blend with the limestone and gneiss. Retracing our steps towards the glacier the way becomes difficult as meltwater washes through the larger boulders and gravel that have been deposited since the retreat of the glacier. There is a state of repose amid the disintegration of rock; time can be seen within a trickle of small weathered shards. Bones lie bleached and clean, reduced to delicate proportions that seem impossibly slender within the harshness of this land. All matter is broken down by winds and the ceaseless cycle of temperature changes.

Looking down on Sombre Lake, the rolling terrain of rock is interspersed by the sleeping forms of fur seals, stirring occasionally to reposition themselves. As I sit within Sombre Hut looking due south across the partially frozen lake I can see my companion as he continues his study of the lake waters. A thin black line describes his path through the fragile ice and by his movements I can see that he is pulling up a tubular chamber of water from the depths of the lake. He is using a white inflatable dingy, giving the impression that he is pulling himself along on a small cushion of ice. Beyond the lake, precipitous combes and gulley glaciers belittle the small figure as he continues his work. It is silent here in the hut except for the sound of contact between pen and paper and the agitated rustle of my waterproof jacket sleeve as it moves across the Formica table top.

The hut is sparsely furnished; a fire extinguisher, paraffin stove, toilet rolls, first aid container and a half empty tub of drinking chocolate accompanied by twelve plastic containers of table salt. The strip light rusts on the ceiling and much of the floor covering of linoleum has been worn away, almost matching the eroded rock surface beyond the open door.

At times the steep rock faces echo to the thunderous sound of avalanches as they cascade from across Borge Bay in the direction of Coronation Island. Frequently the sounds rise from the elephant seals, seeming to come from the deep earth within the bowels of petrified rock.

Unable to return across the 'shallows', we have no choice but to climb Limestone Valley and return to base via the long and circuitous route of the ice cap. The valley is a chaos of fragmenting rock, with numerous streams of meltwater, and we are forced to the valley sides where snow provides surer footing. Once on the upper slopes the snow deepens and we face a stiff breeze. Walking in snow along the high ridge that forms the backbone of Signy is all that I had wanted to do, and now the rhythmic sound of snow being compressed underfoot provides a suitable accompaniment. Soon the guide poles of aluminium rods begin to emerge from the white field before us. To the north Coronation Isle is now blanketed in a low dense cloud, while to the south the great spread of icebergs fade into the distant haze of the Weddell Sea.

10.45 hrs
Limos. (before Snow) Heywood Lake.

Sketch the fourth

> The tilley lamp is lit
> and the hut immediately
> exudes warmth; this is Antarctic,
> and our humble shelter
> on a remote rock
> is truly at the edge
> of our world.

2 February 2003

Signy Island Journal (II)

2 February-3 February 2003. North Point. Foca Hut. 17.30 hrs.

Early evening and a fading light. Across the calm waters of Borge Bay the snow fields of Coronation Island glow in a blue iridescence beneath a cloud cover of steel grey. As we near Foca Hut, Wilson Storm Petrels swoop and dive overhead, and the sounds of the fur seals carry across the metallic surface of a calm sea. Icebergs alternate between greys and silver white as those angled away from the last rays of sunlight are cast into shadow. The tilley lamp is lit and the hut immediately exudes warmth. This is the stage of Antarctica and this humble hut on a remote rock is truly at the edge of our world. From the small window I gaze out onto the sea surface. The smell of paraffin lingers in the upper part of the wooden interior and the sound of the tilley lamp and stove enwraps us in this simple shelter.

3 February. 2003

7.30 hrs. The small windows by our bunk beds are misted over from our night's sleep; through the lower section of glass I can identify the falling of snow. Mist shrouds the details of the nearby headland of rock.

From my bunk I study the hut's interior; daylight exposes more detail than was visible in the dying light of last night. Upon the wooden shelves beneath the end window are two old alarm clocks showing different times. Sheepskins are draped over the spare bunk and a pair of binoculars rests on the window ledge in readiness for the setting of sun and the rising of moon. The whole interior has a comfort of wood. Along the sides of the hut the growing light of day is defining the detail of shelves and cabinets. Elongated windows provide views along the coast towards North Point, though pulses of snow and mist fleetingly obscure the view. As I look up I observe a line of petrel feathers that have been placed in the wooden struts of the roof near to the rusting hook holding the tilley lamp. By the door, beneath a small work surface, stand a number of discarded lamps; some are blackened to a charcoal grey as a result of efforts to light them on earlier occasions.

9.30 hrs. We leave the comfort of the hut and walk through the mist and snow towards North Point, discarding the heavy rucksacks at a large rock by Spindrift Ridge from whence we shall later make tracks back to base camp.

Once at North Point we begin our gentoo penguin count, checking the number of chicks before their departure to sea. I sit within the amphitheatre hollow that forms the beach. Looking across to Coronation Island, the cloud cover now hangs low over the water, touching the tops of the large icebergs. The dark shores of the larger island can be discerned as a soft grey blur of promontories.

The day begins to lighten.

Sketch the fifth

The Polar Hut
is still as English
as that of
Scott at Cape Evans,
with their air of
an early twentieth-century pantry.

They are a world
of past moments
as frozen in time
as the ice
beyond their doors.

4 February 2003

Signy Island Journal (III)

4 February 2003. Gourlay Peninsula.

The walk to Gourlay assumes a pattern: the path is now worn, it is familiar and the partially covered footprints in the snow tell of previous journeys. As I enter the lower slopes of the McLeod Glacier beneath the tower of Garnet Hill I look east over a wide expanse of sea littered with icebergs. Days begin to revolve around a play of scale as I compare the bergs to known objects.

The snow is soft. Beneath the crystals of cornice snow hard ice gleams out. My ski pole strikes an impenetrable solid with a thud and I skid across areas of slush and hard ice, trying to avoid the danger of crevasses.

Once at the base of Gourlay snow slope I imagine known points to my right and left: Lenton Point and Rethval. These earlier visits have now formed part of the mental map, they have been absorbed and stored away. This process of assimilation gathers elements of control within these remote places. Territory is consumed within the memory.

15.00 hrs. I sit within Gourlay Hut. A strengthening wind is picking up and a light fall of sleet blows across the peninsula. Above the sound of the wind the incessant calls rise from the chinstrap penguins; their nesting areas are spread over the nearby rocks and headlands. A surface of regurgitated krill and droppings carpets the mid distance in a pink splash of colour, sending a pungent stench of ammonia into the breeze.

In the bay below a large berg of blue-grey ice has become snagged on the rocks and is now static. I walk to the water's edge to study its surface. It is alien and its surface is pitted and shaped by the breaking of waves over its broad back. It is domed and hard with regular indentations spread evenly over its opaque outer skin. Its edges have been rounded by constant wave action, which has also undercut a distinct ledge around its base. The ice mass moves rhythmically within the coastal current, giving the uneasy impression that the rock upon which I stand is in motion, while the ice itself is static. This illusion is soon dispelled as the dome of ice drifts away from the rock; a frozen leviathan carried in the buoyancy of the Southern Ocean.

17.00 hrs. I depart from the hut and walk towards base, heading into a biting wind. Once on the snow slope, I see that much of the old surface has thawed to reveal the blue-black ice beneath, like a bruising upon the purity of snow. From beneath Garnet Hill the scene to the east is one of relentless low cloud and sleet. Sky and sea are merged into one, broken only by the seemingly suspended outlines of the individual icebergs.

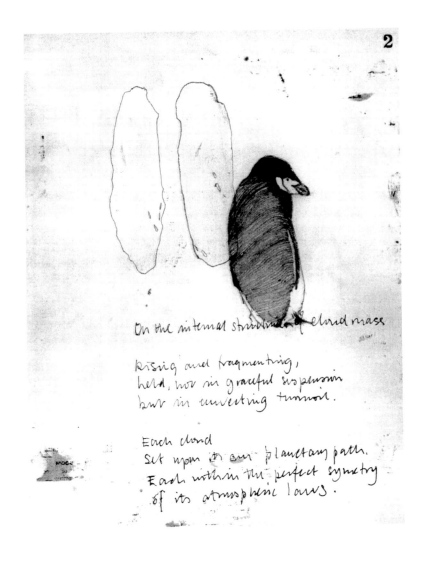

On the internal structure of cloud mass

Rising and fragmenting,
held, not in graceful suspension
but in unresting turmoil.

Each cloud
Set upon its own planetary path,
Each within the perfect symmetry
of its atmospheric laws.

Sketch the sixth

> 'It is not what I saw or
> believed I saw that, in the end,
> is important. It is what I
> thought.'
>
> T. Pynchon

6 February 2003

Signy Island Journal (IV)

6 February 2003. Observation Bluff and Green Cable.

I sit looking due north to Coronation Island, sheltered from the wind by the rocks of Observation Bluff. Much of the larger island is obscured within layers of strato-cumulus cloud and the lower slopes are divided into distinct layers by strips of scud cloud drifting slowly across the rock faces. Sounds rise from the beach below as waves lap against rock and grounded sea ice. Looking down I see fur seals at play in the grey waters. Skywards and the skuas are circling the rock that I have selected to sketch from. A low band of sleet halts my progress at sketching, and Coronation Island becomes veiled in cloud, while the bay and nearby cove become filled with cold precipitation.

Snow replaces sleet, and visibility is further restricted as I climb towards Rusty Bluff. These rocky hills have become established in my mind as the 'tops' in the growing familiarity of this strange landscape.

16.30 hrs. The cloud level has now dropped upon the cold waters as I sit on the rocks close to the island's beacon. Across the leaden waters Coronation Island is all but lost in the thick veil of swirling air, and, with the exception of one area of light, all details of the coast are gone. Icebergs, grounded upon the sea bed fade into mid distance; milky, cloud-like blurs of light. Those closer to the Signy shore reveal their large areas of sub-surface ice, blue and silent within the chill waters.

The thickening gloom of the low cloud cover adds to the sense of isolation; the way to the north has been smothered by this curtain of air, and I feel the distances beyond the island that I can no longer see. The hold of Antarctica grips and absorbs all the still air. I sit isolated on this lonely rock surrounded by the creature sounds that are dispatched into white infinity.

Sketch the seventh

> In these moments, infinite space,
> endless ether
> and timeless silence
> smother thought
>
> with a strange
> unaccountable sensation
> of departure and ascent.

9 February 2003

Signy Island Journal (V)

9 February 2003. Garnet Hill and Moraine Valley.

A dense low cloud fills the valley, erasing the upper crags as a thin veil of convecting air descends and disperses upon the rocky slopes. At the head of the valley I look towards Garnet Hill as it appears fleetingly in a break of cloud. A thaw is in motion and the urgent sounds of meltwater carry across the white surface; much of the snow slope is now a mat of blue-grey bloom and the sheet movement of the water is mapped vividly upon the cold surface.

High upon the piedmont of Rusty Bluff I sit and draw the rock debris. The mist thickens, low cloud removes all sight of Garnet Hill, and I find myself enveloped within a white ocean of air.

Only the purity of the remaining snow surface gives any definition or sense of distance; elsewhere, vague grey outlines, stabbed with the occasional piercing light of snow patch and hard ice. These are the moments when Antarctica becomes ascendant and re-imposes its presence. In these moments infinite space, endless ether and timeless silence smother thought with the strange, unaccountable sensation of departure and ascent. I am filled with strange, unutterable feelings, as the pervading silence becomes urgent. I could look at this whiteness with its faintness of touch, detail of ice crystal and snow about my feet for eternity. Here, on the snow slope, a journey's end but for the brief impulse to make fresh prints in the snow. My sequence of thought is broken by the simple path of flight of an Antarctic Tern: the black head and wing motion break the surface serenity that spreads out before me.

14.00 hrs. High on the 'tops' within the clouds, and wherever there is a scattering of bone fragments, so the skuas will be. A ledge of rock like a sacrificial table is littered with the white bones of Cape Petrel and Antarctic Tern. Nearby, a skua eyes me suspiciously; overhead a commotion of wings and the bird's partner returns from the hunt.

Sketch the eighth

> Much that is Antarctic
> concerns 'footprints'.
>
> Impressions in the snow
> the mark of being there
> and
> the gesture of a fleeting contact,
> is all that is left
> in this cold land.

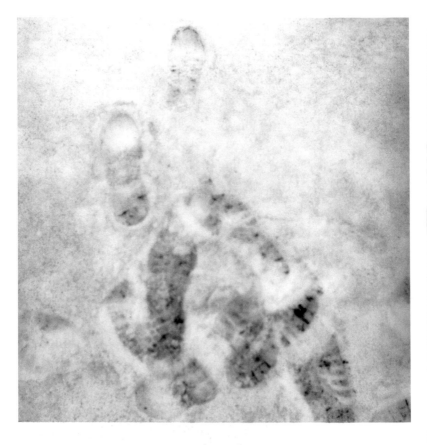

14 February 2003

Signy Island Journal (VI)

14 February 2003. Garnet Hill.

Despair and elation are closely aligned in this place, as glimpses of the sublime are interspersed with the low cloud of gloom. I awake to a brighter day. Overnight the blanket of cloud has dispersed and from base I can see the peaks at Jane Col and Spindrift clearly and sharply defined. Coronation Island, with its higher ground, is still draped in dense cloud above the height of 2,000 feet; however, as is frequently the case, Sunshine Glacier is bathed in early morning light. Recent days of thaw have exposed crevasses on the snow, slope and icecap, making them easier to avoid.

Overnight snow has drifted on the slope that rises to Garnet and occasionally I find myself sinking into the fresh fall that has accumulated between the hard ridges of ice. Following the backbone of rock from the icecap, I am able to ascend to the crest of the hill. Below I can see the small dark figures of Mike and Aki as they make their way down Gourlay slope to the peninsula and the penguin colonies. This lonely island within Antarctica divides into two distinct zones: the low coastal areas and 'flats' teem with life and resound to the calls of seals and birds in flight as well as the constant sound of the penguins, while the high terrain of snow and ice that forms the central spine is almost silent. It is a silence broken only by the sounds of the wind.

Today there is barely any wind at all and I sit enclosed within the weight of this silence, with only the clinkerous chime of rock as I shift my feet to maintain the warmth of circulation. No birds disturb these rock chambers and consequently no bones litter the ground. Grey-brown moss grows tenuously on a fragmented and broken surface of frost-shattered rock, and the slopes look like a rubble of discarded china.

With a glimpse of sunlight on the far slopes of North Signy I glance up into the sky: through the mist and low cloud of stratocumulus I can see the outline of the sun throwing its light down, as if through misted ice, upon Antarctica. I sit within that cold world deep in the chill of circulating air.

13.00 hrs. The general cloud level appears to be descending and snow flurries fill the air. The descending cloud base compresses the silence, condensing it within a narrow band between the level of convection and solid rock. Descending the slopes from Garnet Hill, holes appear within the frozen surface containing fragments of rock that have come from the base of the hill, the depth of hole determined by the drill of gravitation in times of thaw. Once within the confines of Moraine Valley I can see that the descending cloud base has stabilised and now fills the upper air over the Orwell Glacier. Behind me Garnet Hill is clear and hard-edged within the light of early evening.

Sketch the ninth

> Enter
> the white fields of Antarctica
> and
> you
> enter
> into yourself.

15 February 2003

Signy Island Journal (VII)

15 February 2003. Lake survey of the entire island.

18.00 hrs. By the time we reach Cummings Bay the weather has begun to deteriorate, with driving snow and falling temperatures. From Cummings we climb the Gneiss Hills as the violence of the winds make the going very hard. From the driven snow of the exposed ridge we descend onto the McLeod Glacier, put on our crampons and make our way beyond the base of Garnet Hill. Visibility has continued to deteriorate and the light is now fading. We have been in the field for ten hours as we reach Khyber Lake, with the wind rising through Moraine Valley. The last part of our walk will be into the full force of the wind.

Earlier in the day I had pencilled in my sketch book that 'when you go into the white of Antarctica you journey into yourself.' Ten hours later I pull my book from the soaked jacket pocket and in the driving snow, with the page just visible, I write:

'Much self-analysis within Antarctica has to do with the reflective surface of white. Within most landscapes the soft and varied tones, the warmth of vegetation, the fields and the forests, the plains, valleys and mountains all absorb the scope of your imagination, they are receptive. In Antarctica the light of the blank surface is thrown back at you. It reflects upon you, causing introspection. The eye-mind cannot register upon movement or depth of colour; it has to contend with a "nothingness", an infinity. It is the intimidation of a white canvas and the fear of a blank page.'

Sketch the tenth

Sometimes life at Signy feels as if we exist
under water. Low cloud, the deadening mist, the
great circulation of the polar air and the melt
of the glaciers all conspire within the immense
systems of the earth.

18 February 2003

Signy Island Journal (VIII)

18 February 2003. Gourlay Penninsula and Lenton Point.

Early fog disperses along the hard contours of Jane Peak. The day is windless and from the top of the stone ridge the Orwell Glacier can be seen piercing the mist as snow absorbs the warmth of sunlight. There is absolute silence; no bird calls and the recumbent fur seals are motionless and quiet. Glacier and snow patch are reflected in the meltpools, producing a strange inverted world seen through the thin surface ice remaining from the frozen hours before dawn.

11.00 hrs. At Khyber Lake the rock mass of Garnet Hill is but a dark smudge seen through the lingering mist. There are sounds of glacial melt filling the upper valley. Soon the great circulation of waters will cease and Antarctica will stand still within the long winter months before unleashing its waters to the world of the north. As I walk across the Gourlay Snow Slope I am accompanied by the sound of breaking ice underfoot.

12.00 hrs. At Lenton Point I sit and look out over the grey waters towards the distant accumulation of icebergs. At one time these waters would have held the great leviathans, their scale matching that of the sections of ice shelf that now drift in front of me. With their dreadful yet magnificent presence gone, the sense of loss is almost tangible.

15.00 hrs. At Gourlay I pick up the small, flat whitened stones from the abandoned resting areas of the chinstrap penguins. A coinage, and with it the soft down left by the young chicks as they made their way to the sea. The small feathers retain their heat in my closed hand. As I sit within Gourlay Hut lost in thought and drifting to the incessant noise of the penguins, I slip into that mood of introspection, wrapped within the soft contours of snow.

Sketch the eleventh

Like the breaking of a spell, our inaccessibility
is suddenly exposed as a delusion. Yet, in being
protective towards our island home we had recognised our
affection for this place of ice, snow and mist.
The chatter of strangers' voices in the corridors of the base
building; the high pitch of outboard motors in
the bay, and the sight of kayaks littered across
the waters where the fur seals swim and play.

Yet Signy is inviolate and slips back easily into
the peaceful rhythms that have existed here for
millions of years. These encounters are fleeting
and their memory fades into the cold of the polar
evening. The disturbed waters become calm and the
sound is once again 'oceanic'.

19 February 2003. Visit of the tourist ship, *Endeavour*, to Signy
Island, South Orkney.

Signy Island Journal (IX)

20 February 2003. Jane Col and Limestone Valley.

10.30 hrs. I ascend the limestone valley to Jane Col and enter the lower stratocumulus cloud before reaching the work hut that serves as a meteorological centre and recording point. As I enter the hut the sound of the generator propeller can be heard from its attachment on the roof. Once inside I take note of the contents—wooden pegs, a primus stove with working instructions, ropes, a selection of tools, a tin of methylated spirits and a hard-frozen emergency mars bar.

A circuitous route around the hut reveals the geological history of this remote col. In the scattered stones are stories of sea bed accumulation, upheaval and the force of compaction. Long shards of rock indicate the route of earlier glaciers as they ground their way down to the west coast to be dispersed into the immensity of the Southern Ocean. The action of frost has broken rocks down to a fine mosaic pavement that trails from where I stand into the mid distance, producing a sheen of fine grey. Fragments of rock are patterned as if by some early plant remains, forming a pottery of fronds that give an intelligence to this exposed and uncompromising place. All the tortuous history of rock now lies scattered within the gentle valley slopes held in the silence of this day.

15.00 hrs. Throughout the day the collapse of snow and ice carries sound across the straits from Coronation Island; a rumbling storm and an omen of change.

20.00 hrs. In the evening I observe the dying light of the day. Silent now, the snow and ice have become stabilised by the hold of falling temperatures in a grip of ice crystals. Sitting on the wooden verandah of the base building, I feel an overwhelming sensation of being a fleeting visitor—of passing through—that all around me is so much of its own relentless order.

Sketch the twelfth

> The white expanse of Antarctica encourages a
> process of elimination. Thought and reality are
> separated by the thinnest of layers, as if the
> landscape itself has entered our mind's way.
>
> Thoughts come as if lifted from the surfaces
> of snow, but we can only struggle to assert
> some intelligence against the forces of these
> brutal lands.

22 February 2003

'It gives me great pleasure to see nature in these great, though terrible scenes. It fills the mind with grand ideas and turns the soul upon itself.'

Edmund Burke, *A Philosophical Enquiry into the Origin of our Ideas of the Sublime and Beautiful*, 1757.

Signy Island Journal (X)

22 February 2003. Cummings Cove.

11.00 hrs. Crossing the ice cap we descend to Cummings Cove. This vast, remote amphitheatre of metamorphic rock has been denuded extensively to produce an area of fragmentation. Over the passage of time these incessant processes have created a debris of scree and traced a tapestry of paths traversing the land and leading to the cold margin of the ice sea.

16.00 hrs. At that margin stands Cummings Hut, and having completed a penguin count with Mike I am to 'overnight' with Richard. Soon the tilley lamps and the stove are lit and the hut is transformed from a cold, bleak outpost to a warm shelter. I collect sea ice to melt down for a cup of tea and we sit while the interior of the hut warms us.

18.30 hrs. I leave the warmth of the hut to search along the coast for remains and rocks; earlier, the remains of a large penguin had been seen near the fur seals, and I soon find the partly decomposed body. It is a king penguin and I am able to retrieve the skull for my collection; it is a fine specimen.

20.00 hrs. In the final light of the day, guided by the iridescent glow from the ice and snow I make my way back to the safety of the hut. From the beach I gaze back at the small stone shelter and the warmth of light coming from the tilley lamp through the small window. A single beacon within a bleak and cold landscape. Once inside the hut all the cold of the dark night is forgotten; occasionally the thunder of ice collapsing at sea returns our thoughts to the reality of our geographical position and throughout the night the deep muffled drumming of ice upon ice carries over the skin of the ocean.

Sketch the thirteenth

In the fading light of the day the mist cleared
and the glaciers and ice cap of Coronation Island
glowed within their cold world.

Above the peaks an ominous cloud formation of
spiralling black convection rose up to the outer
limits of the troposphere.

26 February 2003

Signy Island Journal (XI)

26 February 2003. Three Lakes Valley and the Ice Cap.

Those omens of the sky proved to be true as we wake to a ferocious wind and driving snow. It is the day of the seal count and Mike and I are to cover the Three Lakes area.

9.00 hrs. We ascend the stone slope and make our way to the shallows to catch the tide. The surge of water produced by the wind has influenced the tidal flow in the Southern Ocean to the extent that we cannot attempt the crossing. Huddled amongst the rocks of Cemetery Flats we wait for low water and eventually attempt a crossing; half way across and we abandon the efforts to step from stone to stone and wade the final section. With wet feet we set forward walking into winds of 60 mph as sleet and snow sting our faces.

12.30 hrs. We reach the shelter of Sombre Hut and sit inside; wind buffets the simple structure so that we have to raise our conversation to shouting disconnected calls on the absurdity of our task. Looking through the steamed-up window I can see waterspouts rising from Stigen Beach, while in the other direction I can see the extent of the falling sleet and snow against the black backdrop of the mountains leading to the Ice Cap. Soon we will have to climb those slopes and traverse the ice to get back to base.

13.30 hrs. Having reached the heights of Jane Col, we put our crampons on and continue to the steep slope of Snow Hills. Assisted by the force of adrenaline, we reach the top in winds that are now gusting at force 12. Ice debris is being carried along the surface and is striking us below waist level. Once at Snow Hills, in the lee of the ridge, we are able to rest; visibility is still good and we can make out the line of poles that indicate our route towards Garnet Hill and the southern section of the ridge. Once we have achieved the highest point of the cap the wind is full behind us and we are able to descend with more control.

At Khyber we sit again, taking advantage of the large rock that I frequently use when coming from the exposure of the ice cap. It is at these moments that the song of Antarctica is clearest. Following a sustained period of physical exertion comes the chance for reflection and:

> 'the realisation that Antarctica has always been so, throughout the geological ages, changing little and relentless in its seasons. Regardless of what we interpret

in the deeper minds of men, we visit, we observe, we depart and we endure. As I sit now within the warmth of base office I look out on a scene of violent force...a tide of brash ice is being thrown against the slipway that leads to the two inflatable rafts and these boats are now encircled within a group of broken bergs. Visibility is fading and the ocean surface is alive to the energy of the rising storm. No longer can I see the heights over which we struggled earlier in the day. The transition from physical exertion to a mental peace is now complete and the day is passing, but in the dark chambers of the mind is the deadening realisation of the routines within the world to which we must return.'

All that is left of the day is a catalogue of weather conditions...

Winds...strong to hurricane force.
Temperature...2 to -10 degrees Celsius.
Cloud...total sky coverage, low cumulus.
Visibility...deteriorating throughout the day.

This day in Maritime Antarctica, Signy Island was buffeted by the Southern Ocean along its cold and windswept shores and beaches. A day when the thaw of the Ice Cap was halted by the force of a South Atlantic storm...and when two, small figures may have been seen crossing the heights of the Island.

Sketch the fourteenth

    Columns of spiralling snow on the ice cap
    are seen clearly against the dark sky
    beyond.

    The sound of an incoming tide
    of brash ice
    sounds,
    like a frozen shingle
    upon a storm beach.

28 February 2003

Signy Island Journal (XII)

28 February 2003. Tioga Hill and the Ice Cap.

With good visibility, I decide to take the opportunity to climb the Ice Cap and Tioga Hill, which forms the highest point of the island. Winds are still exceeding 30 knots as I depart from base.

11.00 hrs. Reaching the triangle of poles marking the intersection of routes that cross the Ice Cap, I look over towards Coronation Island. The distant mountains are shrouded in a low cloud and violent föhn winds cascading down its steep glaciated slopes are creating convection storms. On Signy visibility is still good, though winds have strengthened and the surrounding snow slopes are vague with the blown snow lifting from their surfaces. I sit within a small rocky outcrop that forms the eastern extension of the Everson Ridge and am able to sketch within its shelter. Tioga Hill lies approximately half a mile to the west.

With the wind behind me I walk across fresh snow to Tioga and climb to the small stone cairn that marks the highest point: the chill within the wind only allows a quick sketch before returning to my shelter within the rock outcrop. As I look to the south I notice how still the expanse of sea appears, despite the gusting winds. The distant growlers and brash ice appear like white breakers in a dark ocean. Looking at the larger icebergs it is possible to read their individual history; some have retained their tabular forms, others have tilted in a moment of calamitous fall and retained only a slight reminder of their original shape. For some these moments of collapse and fragmentation are held in time by the ice and gradually their white contours are being softened by the action of salt water as it flows along their flanks.

14.00 hrs. Returning towards Garnet Hill, I notice that the drift snow has filled my footsteps producing white imprints across the hard ice surface. This surface is now frozen, resisting, temporarily, my weight upon its brittle cornice. There is no sound of meltwater and the energetic flow of water within the deep cut channels has become static beneath a covering of freshly fallen snow. Looking east towards the foothills of Rusty Bluff great slopes of scree fan out from below the sheer crags and are now being transformed to a light grey shingle by the ice and snow.

Sketch the fifteenth

> Antarctica symbolises
> on a scale like
> no other place on earth
>
> the innate desire
> of man to tread
> on new ground.

1230 hrs
Jlw to Fora Hur and
the west coast; much
sea ice n Filled Fora Bay.
hght Lake

2 March 2003

Signy Island Journal (XIII)

2nd March 2003. The Ice Cap.

In Antarctica moods and states of mind change rapidly, as if in sympathy with the dramatic weather patterns. Moments of gloom and high emotion fluctuate throughout the day.

10.00 hrs. I ascend the backslope from base, avoiding the slippery path of the stone gulley and notice that much blue ice now fills Factory Cove. From Observation Hill to the north-west of Signy and the Pomona Plateau of Coronation Island there is a scene of winter: March within Antarctica signals the autumn and before me I can see brash ice filling the coves and fresh snow deepening on the gentle slopes. Thus it is that the land slips towards the static hold of winter. From Garnet Hill a squall of snow tracks towards Signy from the south-east, consuming icebergs and sea ice as it rolls over the grey surface of the ocean. As it nears the land its course takes to the south, deflected by the rock mass of the Gourlay Peninsula.

11.00 hrs. I make my way to the ice cap, to the rhythmic sounds of ice and snow trodden underfoot. Once upon the high ridge I track to the head of the Orwell Glacier, which forms a no-man's land of shifting ice perilously close to the gaping hazards of the crevasses. The dreadful slope of the glacier head plunges down beyond my line of vision, a cataract of ice falling into Moraine Valley.

13.00 hrs. Two hours of working on the ice cap are sufficient before the wind chill begins to render my hands incapable of sketching the rock masses that rise from the general level of snow, and I make my way down towards the relative shelter of Gourlay. Coronation Island trails away to the eastern horizon, its coastline fragmenting into a necklace of small rocky islands: Mathews, Steepholm, Skilling and finally Atriceps stand proud in a roll call of great survivors in the face of the overwhelming weather—immense forces of attrition reduce these stalwart rocks.

Was there ever such an exposed and hopeless point on Earth as South Cape, South Orkney, facing the vast Weddell Sea and the gates of Antarctica?

14.00 hrs. I am again struck by the onset of winter; the landscape assumes this seasonal adjustment within an instant. No foliage to wither and fall, only the relentless fragmenting of exposed rock within the crystal air.

Sketch the sixteenth

> Antarctica
> is a place of
> dreams.
>
> I close my eyes
> and I can
> see
> the
> south.

4 March 2003

Signy Island Journal (XIV)

4 March 2003. Gourlay.

11.00 hrs. Absolute silence, but for the 'soussos' of the earth— is that simply an invention for our ears to ease the discomfort of infinity? At the top of the scree gulley there is no wind and a low mank covers the ice cap. An air visible, hanging in its stillness from where I stand to the distant rocks of the valley slopes. A slow walk in snow, treading the new surface like a carpet of the subconscious, throwing up thoughts as casually as refracted light, and entering the other side of silence to a placid space. Swathed in fresh snow, the slopes and the sky become one and rock protuberances appear strangely airborne within the white immensity as I make my way to Gourlay. Pulses of snow reduce visibility at the start of the snowslope, but crampons are unnecessary as my feet sink deep within the snow.

As a child the departure from the sea at the end of the annual holiday to Norfolk had always been a sad event. Gazing through the car's rear window at the fast fading surface of the North Sea had always been difficult. In Antarctica I was now beginning to feel similar emotions; I was looking out of a small window at a fading landscape.

I make my way over the rough terrain to Gourlay hut to retrieve three penguin eggs I had placed there on a previous visit. Once at the hut I sit within the sheepskin covered seat and wedge the door open so that I can see the small inlet that is now full of brash ice, as well as the colonies of penguins lining the headland. Somewhere down on the ice a leopard seal is lying in wait for an unsuspecting penguin. I pick up the three hard shelled eggs and place them on the top of the Formica table.

The thick brash ice moves back and forth within the cove, carried within the lungs of the sea; a great inhalation and exhalation, the source of which lies somewhere out in the open ocean. Within the deep, great leviathans glide in the dark waters.

17.00 hrs. Returning via the heights of Garnet I stand within the great ghosting shape of the hill and bathe in the white totality. Some force is urging me to rise, to go forward into the night and enter that realm of white darkness.

Sketch the seventeenth

> Antarctica,
> in glorious isolation
> upon
> an oceanic planet.
>
> Deserted
> by the drift
> of continents,
> to leave
> this
> solitary,
> white land.

5 March 2003

Signy Island Journal (XV)

5 March 2003. Robin Peak and the Ice Cap.

At the northern tip of Signy, Robin Peak juts out into the Normanna Strait; during my stay I have frequently looked at this particular rock mass in the evening light from Factory Cove. I have seen it in all the tones of early evening and now I stand in bright sunlight upon its peak. A windless day prompted Aki and me to take this opportunity to walk to this part of the island; a boat to Waterpipe Hut and then the climb to Spindrift Col, finally leading to the snowy heights of Northern Point.

Standing at the peak, the silence is absolute and sufficient to hear a whale's breath. Only the low thunder of avalanche and the explosive crack of ice collapse enter the still air for fleeting moments. To the west, through near perfect visibility, spreads the dramatic expanse of the sea ice. Somewhere within the still, grey waters whales swim amid the avenues of ice and the opaline surfaces of the shelves; beneath the expectant air, the sheen of the ocean skin and the depths of the blue world of suspended ice.

14.00 hrs. From Robin Peak we begin to walk along the spine of the island towards Snow Hills. The sunlight upon the ice cap is penetrating a high gauze of cirrus cloud and we stand within its warmth. We look south from the crest of the ice cap to the great tabular icebergs that have broken from the ice shelf. Some are in sunlight and glow in brilliance, while others in shadow are as dark as the sea surface.

15.00 hrs. A grey layer of cumulus cloud edges northwards, sending a dark, leaden surface over the sea; the waters in Borge Bay assume a dull surface like estuary mud. Snow now falls upon the still waters.

Sketch the eighteenth

Antarctica is cold and lifeless, ageing slowly within
the great systems that circulate around the polar area.
For the past six weeks I have placed myself against its power,
searching for reason and cataloguing individual
moments in the hope of attaining something from the
encounter. I suspect that given many lifetimes I could
not achieve more than this.

6 March 2003

Signy Island Journals (XVI)

6 March 2003. The Ice Cap.

14.00 hrs. On this 'dingle' day the last breezes of summer blow from the south. Sitting at Garnet Hill I am blinded by the sunlight on the ice. Walking in snow and being in Antarctica was all that I had wanted and now, with departure fast approaching, I try to assess the weeks spent within the south. I am drawn to the landscape. The complex dialogues between landscape and man cannot be entirely unravelled; our interaction with place initiates an infinite number of responses.

As if to prolong my stay I walk further upon the ice cap, not wishing to return to the lower slopes. All I can do is stand within the snow and gaze about me, happy to breathe in the chill air and bathe in the glare of reflected sunlight.

19.30 hrs. Sitting outside base upon the wooden bench, I am joined by one of the skuas that feed on the scraps of food. I sit here amid the sound of the incoming tide as it washes against the jetty. Soon the prions will start their chatter from the nearby rocks and from beneath the wooden eaves of the base building. The chill in the air clamps down on the snowfields that I see about me as the skua flies off over the dark waters, returning to her nesting area on the backslope. Ahead of me the hard rock outlines of Jane Peak and Robin Bluff are still clear in the twilight.

There is light in the sky, but no moon or stars; such are the night skies in the southern polar region. Soon the outlines of peak and glacier will fade into the black night and any stars will be obscured beyond the weight of cloud.

20.00 hrs. The last light fades upon the brooding outlines of Antarctica.

Sketch the nineteenth

> Glancing from the office window
> I look at the Signy map on the wall.
> It appears small, contained and
> familiar, like an old friend, as I
> contemplate the voyage out from the
> shelter of these islands into the
> open waters of the South Atlantic.

7 March 2003

Signy Island Journal (XVII)

7 March 2003. Departure from Signy.

The day of departure and I rise at 6.00 for 'gash' duties, which I do without my customary list of instructions. All the fine weather of the past two days has gone and as I make my way to the generator shed I am met with a curtain of snow lifted in a rising wind. Brash ice has been blown into the bay and characteristically a cluster of small bergs surround the two inflatable dinghies that are being jostled in the grey waters beyond the jetty.

News from the 'Shack' is positive and we should be on board by mid-morning. As I sit in the office the computer screen throws up an image that looks like a coastline and an immense area of sea: white flecks are being detached and drift towards the blue of the sea before disappearing. It seems to be an archetypal model of the Antarctic Peninsula and strangely forewarns of the hazards within the ocean.

10.00 hrs. The RRS *Ernest Shackleton* arrives and despatches a small craft that threads its way through the ice to deliver two personnel and to pick up the four who are leaving. Once we have secured our lifebelts and jackets we are off, and skim over a rough sea into the snowstorm. Salt water and ice crystals strike my face, and by the time we pull along side of the ship my hands are frozen to a bright red and blue patchwork.

14.00 hrs. From the bridge I look back at Signy. Deteriorating weather has reduced the island to vague outlines as the light on Beacon Rock pierces the gloom from the heights of the backslope. I can recognise the dim grey mass of Rusty Bluff and from the direction of the ice cap a pale light rises into the weight of the cloud cover.

19.00 hrs. Making my way to the upper deck I look towards Signy and can still make out a dark shape through the gloom. As night descends so the beams of light from the ship illuminate the immediate waters as we move on and manoeuvre our passage through the icebergs. I look at the great walls of ice drifting within the grey waters and realise that Signy has now gone from view and disappeared into the cold black distance of the polar night.

Days at Sea (III)

7-10 March 2003

Days at Sea (IV)

8th March 2003. The South Scotia Sea.

The spell of the Southern Ocean holds us once more as we head north through the ice sea. As I read the various publications on life in these waters, it becomes increasingly clear that much of the mystery is fed by the rarity of certain sightings. Many species of fish have, in all probability, never been seen by man. In the hadal regions of the deep sea there are beings that live in darkness and are completely sightless.

On the rarity of sightings I come across the history of the Lagenorhynchus Cruciger. That a comparatively common dolphin

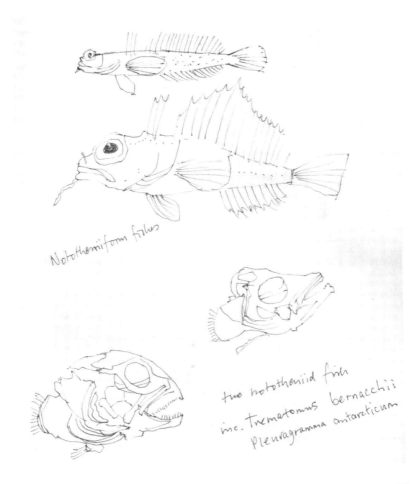

Notothen4form fishes

two notothenid fish
inc. Trematomus bernacchii
Pleuragramma antarcticum

may only be sighted occasionally suggests that much of the life in these vast waters is still unknown to us.

LAGENORHYNCHUS CRUCIGER

The first record of this fish was during a voyage of the Uraine and Physicienne in 1817-20. Dolphin were sighted and though not caught, pictures were drawn, which by a comparison with recent photographs, indicate the uncertainty of sight recordings. By 1960 only three species of this dolphin had been examined; nevertheless, this appears to have been the 'cruciger dolphin'.

A recent record from a vessel of Balaena's whaling fleet... 'Log entry 12.3.58. On a calm ocean with one or two icebergs in sight, position 55 24'S 13 58'E we shot a whale. Once shot, the whale attracted a number of fish and included the crucigers, as the whale was being winched in.'

Days at Sea (V)

'I remember the first albatross I ever saw. It was during a prolonged gale, in waters hard upon the Antarctic seas. From my forenoon watch below, I ascended to the overcrowded deck and there, dashed upon the main hatches, I saw a regal, feathery thing of unspotted whiteness, and with a hooked, Roman bill sublime. At intervals it arched forth its vast archangel wings, as if to embrace some holy ark. Wondrous flutterings and throbbings shook it. Though bodily unharmed, it uttered cries, as some King's ghost in supernatural distress. Through its inexpressible, strange eyes, me thought I peeped to secrets which took hold of God. As Abraham before the angels, I bowed myself; the white thing was so white, its wings so wide, and in those for ever exiled waters, I had lost the miserable warping memories of traditions and of towns. Long I gazed at that prodigy of plumage. I cannot tell, can only hint, the things that darted through me then.'

Herman Melville, *Moby Dick*

Days at Sea (VI)

10 March 2003, Drake Passage.

All day, in seas of 30-40 foot
waves, I lay on my bunk and
breathed to the rhythm of the ship.
At night the beams of light
illuminated the white icy waters,
fixing occasionally on a wall of ice
and the dimensions of the berg.
Through the storm did we voyage—

to enter that silent sea of our
imagination. As a sanctity in
that vast and turbulent ocean,
we departed this physical world
to the calm within our minds,
as haven to the screaming wind,
where dreams and hopes sustained us.

As I lay I dwelt upon the
circular nature of the storm,
as we passed through pulses
from its central power, back
to calmer waters; imagining
the great swirling body of
air above us, pulling the
water of the sea in its train.
A tempest,
and we within it,
part of the great convecting
mass,
deep within the restless
ocean of air.

Eventually,
sleep, and entry to that
silent sea.
Within the motion of the sea,
becoming familiar in its

muscular pitch and roll.
Reading its wild waters
to discern a sequence
and a song,
a great breathing rhythm
orchestrated from the
spinning air
above.